WOMEN
AND
WORK
IN THE OLD TESTAMENT

THEOLOGY OF WORK   PROJECT

WOMEN
AND
WORK
IN THE OLD TESTAMENT

THE BIBLE AND YOUR WORK
Study Series

HENDRICKSON
PUBLISHERS

Theology of Work, The Bible and Your Work Study Series: Women and Work in the Old Testament

© 2015 by Hendrickson Publishers Marketing, LLC
P.O. Box 3473
Peabody, Massachusetts 01961-3473

ISBN 978-1-61970-673-6

Adapted from the *Theology of Work Bible Commentary*, copyright © 2014 by the Theology of Work Project, Inc. All rights reserved.

William Messenger, Executive Editor, Theology of Work Project
Sean McDonough, Biblical Editor, Theology of Work Project
Patricia Anders, Editorial Director, Hendrickson Publishers

Contributor:

Alice Mathews, "Women and Work in the Old Testament" Bible Study

The Theology of Work Project is an independent, international organization dedicated to researching, writing, and distributing materials with a biblical perspective on work. The Project's primary mission is to produce resources covering every book of the Bible plus major topics in today's workplaces. Wherever possible, the Project collaborates with other faith-and-work organizations, churches, universities and seminaries to help equip people for meaningful, productive work of every kind.

Printed in the United States of America

First Printing—December 2015

Contents

The Theology of Work

Work is not only a human calling, but also a divine one. "In the beginning God created the heavens and the earth." God worked to create us and created us to work. "The LORD God took the man and put him in the garden of Eden to till it and keep it" (Gen. 2:15). God also created work to be good, even if it's hard to see in a fallen world. To this day, God calls us to work to support ourselves and to serve others (Eph. 4:28).

Work can accomplish many of God's purposes for our lives—the basic necessities of food and shelter, as well as a sense of fulfillment and joy. Our work can create ways to help people thrive; it can discover the depths of God's creation; and it can bring us into wonderful relationships with co-workers and those who benefit from our work (customers, clients, patients, and so forth).

Yet many people face drudgery, boredom, or exploitation at work. We have bad bosses, hostile relationships, and unfriendly work environments. Our work seems useless, unappreciated, faulty, frustrating. We don't get paid enough. We get stuck in dead-end jobs or laid off or fired. We fail. Our skills become obsolete. It's a struggle just to make ends meet. But how can this be if God created work to be good—and what can we do about it? God's answers for these questions must be somewhere in the Bible, but where?

The Theology of Work Project's mission has been to study what the Bible says about work and to develop resources to apply the

Christian faith to our work. It turns out that every book of the Bible gives practical, relevant guidance that can help us do our jobs better, improve our relationships at work, support ourselves, serve others more effectively, and find meaning and value in our work. The Bible shows us how to live all of life—including work—in Christ. Only in Jesus can we and our work be transformed to become the blessing it was always meant to be.

To put it another way, if we are not following Christ during the 100,000 hours of our lives that we spend at work, are we really following Christ? Our lives are more than just one day a week at church. The fact is that God cares about our life *every day of the week*. But how do we become equipped to follow Jesus at work? In the same ways we become equipped for every aspect of life in Christ—listening to sermons, modeling our lives on others' examples, praying for God's guidance, and most of all by studying the Bible and putting it into practice.

This Theology of Work series contains a variety of books to help you apply the Scriptures and Christian faith to your work. This Bible study is one volume in the series The Bible and Your Work. It is intended for those who want to explore what the Bible says about work and how to apply it to their work in positive, practical ways. Although it can be used for individual study, Bible study is especially effective with a group of people committed to practicing what they read in Scripture. In this way, we gain from one another's perspectives and are encouraged to actually *do* what we read in Scripture. Because of the direct focus on work, The Bible and Your Work studies are especially suited for Bible studies *at* work or *with* other people in similar occupations. The following lessons are designed for thirty-minute lunch breaks (or perhaps breakfast before work) during a five-day work week.

Christians today recognize God's calling to us in and through our work—for ourselves and for those whom we serve. May God use this book to help you follow Christ in every sphere of life and work.

Will Messenger, Executive Editor
Theology of Work Project

Introduction to Women and Work in the Old Testament

The sociological term "patriarchy" originally came from the Greek words *pater* (meaning "father") and *archon* (meaning "ruler"), which together mean "father-rule." Its contrasting term is "matriarchy," meaning "mother-rule." In first-century Roman society, when a mother gave birth to a baby, after eight days the infant was laid at the feet of the father. It was he who then made the decision whether the child would be kept in the family or left in a public place to die (see Lynn Cohick, *Women in the World of the Earliest Christians*). In more recent times the word *patriarchy* has morphed to include any group in which power is held primarily by adult men.

Whatever meaning it has carried in one era or another, the word *patriarchy* describes the dominant structuring of societies almost from the beginning of time. We meet it for the first time in Genesis 3:16: "To the woman [God] said, '. . . your desire shall be for your husband, and he shall rule over you.'" We then see it in action in Genesis 4:19 as Lamech takes two wives (the beginning of polygamy, the ownership of wives). In *Genesis in Space and Time*, Francis Schaeffer reminds us that sin always moves civilizations toward hierarchy. So after the flood (Gen. 7), we find hierarchy among brothers and their descendants: Ham and his descendants will be slaves to his brothers and their descendants (Gen. 9:25–27).

This, however, was not God's original design for those who bear the divine image. Genesis 1:26–28 lays out God's decision to create humanity as male and female in the divine image and likeness, and gives both the man and the woman two tasks: to populate the earth and steward it. Men and women were created to work together, each bringing unique abilities to the team.

Wherever we see hierarchies, we see one group dominating another group, with the history of the dominant group being preserved and the history of the dominated group being ignored. When patriarchy changed the original relationship of the woman to the man, women's stories in virtually all patriarchal societies dropped out of sight.

But the Bible has preserved many of those stories for our benefit. This Bible study focuses on remarkable women in the ancient Near East who mirrored God's values and goals in their actions. Chapter 1 in this study explores how the problem arose, but from chapter 2 through the rest of the study, we follow women who, in one way or another, overturned patriarchal assumptions for the benefit of humanity. It turns out that they are *ezer* women (Gen. 2:18, 20), "helpers" to men who need their help. Thinking about their stories can help us shape our own stories to mirror God's purposes more closely in every corner of our lives and work.

Chapter 1

Men and Women Working Together

Lesson #1: The Importance of Women in the Workplace (Genesis 1:26–31)

From time immemorial, men and women have worked together in whatever workplace they've found themselves. Records reveal that in the early American colonies, women worked at every kind of task from attorneys to undertakers, from blacksmiths to gunsmiths, from jailers to shipbuilders, from butchers to loggers. Some historians tell us that women ran ferries and operated sawmills and gristmills. They ground eyeglasses and painted houses. Every kind of work done by men was done, at least occasionally, by women. Wives had a good knowledge of their husbands' work and often took over the business and ran it successfully when the husband died.

But with the coming of the Industrial Revolution in the 1800s, men's "work" and women's "work" became increasingly separated, so that by the early nineteenth century the "Doctrine of Separate Spheres" was firmly entrenched in people's thinking. Men and women were so different from each other that there could be no overlap in their skills or occupations. In "The Princess" (Part V), English poet laureate Alfred, Lord Tennyson captured this "doctrine" in these words:

Man for the field and woman for the hearth:
Man for the sword and for the needle she:

Man with the head and woman with the heart:
Man to command and woman to obey;
All else confusion.

But that was not God's original design. In Genesis 1:26–28 we read:

> Then God said, "Let us make humankind in our image, according
> to our likeness; and let them have dominion over the fish of the
> sea, and over the birds of the air, and over the cattle, and over all
> the wild animals of the earth, and over every creeping thing that
> creeps upon the earth."

> So God created humankind in his image,
>   in the image of God he created them;
>   male and female he created them.

> God blessed them, and God said to them, "Be fruitful and multiply,
> and fill the earth and subdue it; and have dominion over the fish
> of the sea and over the birds of the air and over every living thing
> that moves upon the earth."

Note that in creating us as male and female, God gave us two
tasks: to create families to populate the earth; and to subdue the
earth, or more accurately, to be stewards or caretakers of God's
creation. Note that these commands are given to both men and
women. Frequently, some folks have assumed that the first command (about the family) was given only to the woman and the
second command (to steward the earth) was given only to the man.
But God gave *both* commands to *both* the man and the woman.
This tells us that men have family responsibilities and that women
have responsibilities to the wider world, as well as to their homes.

This can create tensions for many women, particularly those already burdened with the task of juggling a job outside the home
while caring for a family. Sometimes women are told that their
place is exclusively in the home. But most women who work do
so out of economic necessity: they are either their sole source of
support or their spouse is un- or underemployed. The majority of

working women are not in the workplace so they can buy designer clothes or drive expensive cars. They work to pay the rent or mortgage and put food on the table and shoes on their children's feet.

But women also need to engage the world outside their homes because they bring unique gifts to the workplace. They often bring ideas and ways of thinking to workplace decisions that augment or complement the ideas men bring. Some of the best decision-making comes out of the synergy of these differences as men and women work together.

We might say that it was a brilliant stroke when God created us as male and female and gave us tasks in both the family and the wider world. We complement each other, not by remaining in "separate spheres," but in the convergence of our different gifts.

So the first lesson we learn about women in the Bible is that they are workers, partners with men in the many tasks of stewarding God's creation. Women as well as men are needed in that world for their unique perspectives and gifts.

 Food for Thought

As you think about your roles at work and in the other aspects of life, what problems does having multiple roles cause for you?

_____

_____

_____

_____

_____

Do you think women and men face different issues in the interplay of work and the rest of life, or are the issues the same for men and women?

_____

_____

_____

_____

_____

_____

_____

As you look at yourself in your workplace role, what do you see as your most significant contributions? Do they have anything to do with being female or male?

_____

_____

_____

_____

_____

_____

_____

_____

Lesson #2: Created in God's Image (Genesis 5:1–2)

> God said, "Let us make humankind in our image, according to our likeness." . . . So God created humankind in his image, in the image of God he created them.

What does it mean to be created in God's image and why is it important?

Throughout church history, theologians have come up with different answers to those questions. Early church fathers thought the divine image in us was in our ability to reason. Fifth-century Augustine wrote that the image of God is internal, displayed in the trinity of memory, intellect, and will. Then twelfth-century Thomas Aquinas thought that the image of God in human beings was our "aptitude for understanding and loving God."

More recently, some theologians have defined the image of God as our free will (the power to choose among alternatives). Others focus on our ability to make and sustain human relationships; others add that we have self-awareness. Or that we have a conscience or a sense of "awe." Still others think the image is our aesthetic sense. These are abilities intrinsic to us as human beings.

All of these answers, however, raise an issue we can't ignore: All human beings are created in the divine image, but not all human beings are endowed with equal abilities. Some are born with disabilities that deprive them of memory, intellect, social skills, physical capacity, or other capabilities. So, we must ask if these answers capture the essence of what it means to be "created in the image of God." Have we missed some vital truth about our identity as God's image-bearers?

In Genesis 1:26–27, "Let us make humankind *in* our image," the preposition *in* can also be translated *as*. That choice can make a difference in our understanding of what it means to be created in God's image. Image-bearing is an activity, not just a possession.

N. T. Wright caught this idea in his analogy of an angled mirror. For safety purposes, round concave mirrors are placed at dangerous blind intersections or on narrow mountain roads to reflect information to drivers about unseen oncoming traffic. Like these angled mirrors, Wright suggests that our vocation is to reflect important information about God to those around us.

In our actions and words all of us reflect what we believe about God, whether good or bad. People around us know whether or not we believe that God exists and if we allow God to have some "say" in how we live. The hundreds of choices we make each day—in the workplace or elsewhere—tell the world around us what we really think about God.

Do we agree with the Old Testament prophet Jonah's belief that God is "a gracious God and merciful, slow to anger, and abounding in steadfast love, and ready to relent from punishing" (Jonah 4:2)? If we personally believe that about God, then people will see that image reflected in how we respond to annoying people and events around us. God is gracious; are we? God shows mercy to those deserving punishment; do we? God is slow to anger; are we? God abounds in steadfast, unquenchable love; do we? God is ready to relent from punishing; are we? If so, then we are accurately reflecting God in our daily lives. We are image-bearers who have embraced our vocations as God's representatives here on earth, taking seriously our roles in the workplace as God's "angled mirrors," and communicating to everyone around us who God is.

 Food for Thought

What image of God are you projecting to those around you?

_____

_____

_____

_____

_____

_____

_____

How can you use your God-given abilities to better reflect God to people around you?

_____

_____

_____

_____

_____

Lesson #3: God Creates a Partner for the Man (Genesis 2:18–25)

We've noted in Lesson 1 that in creating us as male and female, God gave us two responsibilities: to create families to populate the earth, and to be stewards or caretakers of God's creation. Both commands came to both the man and the woman.

Now God makes this specific in Genesis 2:18: "Then the LORD God said, 'It is not good that the man should be alone; I will make him a helper as his partner.'" Earlier in Genesis 2, God had put the man in the Garden of Eden with instructions to "till it and keep it" (v. 15). Now in verse 18, a woman is to work alongside this man in that task. But many Christians stumble over the word *helper* as the woman's work assignment. In our day, we use that word to describe someone like a plumber's apprentice, present to hand the plumber the right wrench at the right time. But that is far from the meaning of the Hebrew word used here.

The original Hebrew text calls the woman an *ezer k'negdo*. What do those two words mean? The word *ezer* (translated "helper") occurs twenty-one times in the Old Testament. In two cases is it used for the woman Eve (Gen. 2:18, 20), and three times for nations to whom Israel appealed for military aid (Isa. 30:5; Ezek. 12:14; Dan. 11:34). In the sixteen other cases, it refers to God as our help (see Gen. 2:18, 20; Exod. 18:4; Deut. 33:7, 26, 29; Ps. 20:2; 33:20; 70:5; 89:19; 115:9; 121:1–2; 124:8; 146:5). God is the one who comes alongside us in our helplessness. Because God is not subordinate to his creatures, any idea that an *ezer*-helper is inferior is untenable. In *Man and Woman, One in Christ*, Philip Payne puts it this way:

> The noun used here [*ezer*] throughout the Old Testament does not suggest "helper" as in "servant," but *help, savior, rescuer, protector* as in "God is our help." In no other occurrence in the Old Testament does this refer to an inferior, but always to a superior or an equal; . . . "help" expresses that the woman is a help/strength who rescues or saves man.

While many devout Christians see Eve's function as a subordinate, the word *ezer* cannot support that. Eve was not created to serve Adam, but to serve *with* him. The Hebrew language has other words translated as *helper* that do have the idea of subordination, but none of them was used in Genesis 2:18.

The second Hebrew word in Genesis 2:18 is *k'negdo*, which is translated as "comparable to him" or "suitable to him." The woman is "one fit for him"—in no way a subordinate. Far from referring to a second-string helper handing Adam a shovel, the woman as an *ezer* brings strengths to the man who needs them.

Thus Carolyn Custis James in *Half the Church: Recapturing God's Global Vision for Women* notes that God "deploys the *ezer* to break the man's aloneness by soldiering with him, wholeheartedly and at full strength for God's gracious kingdom. The man needs everything she brings to the global mission."

Without Eve, Adam was only half the story. The woman was not an afterthought or an optional adjunct to an independent, self-sufficient man. God said in Genesis 2:18 that without her Adam's condition was "not good."

The second lesson the Bible teaches us about women is that they are partners with men in the many tasks of stewarding God's creation. But women don't duplicate men; they bring unique gifts needed in their work together. God was clear: It's not good for the man to work alone; he needs an *ezer k'negdo* working with him. As women head to their workplaces each day they go as God's representatives (created in the divine image), called by God as *ezer* women to steward or care for the part of the world in which they work.

 Food for Thought

How do the Hebrew words *ezer* (helper) *k'negdo* (comparable/ suitable to him) change your perspective on the role of women working with men, especially in the workplace?

_____

_____

_____

_____

_____

_____

How might this partnership improve productivity at work?

_____

_____

_____

_____

_____

_____

_____

Prayer

Lord,

We need your help to understand what it means that women are created as an ezer *to men in the workplace. By the power of your Holy Spirit, enable women to be the women you created them to be, and enable men to value what* ezer *women add to their success. We ask this for the sake of your work through us where we work.*

Amen.

Chapter 2

Life Outside Eden: Shiphrah, Puah, and Miriam in a Sin-Filled World

Lesson #1: Sin Invades God's Creation (Genesis 3:16–19)

When Adam and Eve chose to eat some fruit from the garden's forbidden tree, God confronted them with their disobedience. In a blunt conversation recorded in Genesis 3, we learn that the two vocations given to both the man and woman in Genesis 1:28 (peopling the earth and subduing it) would now be made more difficult:

> To the woman he said, "I will greatly increase your pangs in childbearing; in pain you shall bring forth children, yet your desire shall be for your husband, and he shall rule over you." . . . And to the man he said, " . . . cursed is the ground because of you; in toil you shall eat of it all the days of your life; thorns and thistles it shall bring forth for you, and you shall eat the plants of the field. By the sweat of your face you shall eat bread until you return to the ground, for out of it you were taken; you are dust, and to dust you shall return." (Gen. 3:16–19)

Genesis 1 and 2 show us what humanity was created to be; Genesis 3 shows us what humanity chose to become. Both Adam and Eve gained what the serpent promised—a personal knowledge of good and evil. They had known the good in their relationship with God, making the evil they now experienced that much more stark in its awfulness.

What happened to the *ezer* woman Eve was created to be? Would the consequences of her choices affect all women who came after her? Certainly childbirth for women has been more difficult. But what about that line, "Your husband . . . shall rule over you"? Would all women at all times and in all places be forever under a man's rule? And would that change their *ezer* creation? Would they end up as "helpers" in a lesser sense? Or could they still be *ezer* women?

In the early chapters of Genesis we see a jealous brother murdering his sibling, then polygyny entering marriages, then more murders and evil deeds, until in Genesis 6:5 we read that "the LORD saw that the wickedness of humankind was great in the earth, and that every inclination of the thoughts of their hearts was only evil continually." As predicted, life had become difficult for both men and women. It's hard to believe that what had been perfect in the beginning became so evil so quickly. When the situation looked completely hopeless, God chose to wash the world clean in a devastating flood.

Sinful people treat others unjustly. This has been true from the beginning of time and is true today. Both men and women may suffer unjust treatment in the workplace and feel powerless to change their circumstances. But God is aware of that evil and he uses human instruments to challenge its perpetrators. The psalmist knew this:

> Who rises up for me against the wicked? Who stands up for me against evildoers? If the Lord had not been my help [*ezer*], my soul would soon have lived in the land of silence. . . . But the LORD has become my stronghold, and my God the rock of my refuge. He will repay them for their iniquity and wipe them out for their wickedness; the LORD our God will wipe them out. (Ps. 94:16–17, 22–23)

Food for Thought

What difference does it make that God sees evil and will not let it continue forever?

_____

_____

_____

_____

_____

_____

_____

What responsibility might you have in your workplace when you see evildoers harming workers?

_____

_____

_____

_____

_____

_____

_____

_____

Lesson #2: Shiphrah and Puah the *Ezer* Midwives (Exodus 1:15–21)

One consequence of that first sin in the Garden of Eden was women's increased frequency of pregnancies and increased pain in delivering babies (Gen. 3:16). In the midst of this sin-filled world, women continued to give birth. Enter the midwives.

Someone has observed that midwives have been part of the human experience for as long as we have historical records. This particularly female vocation is mentioned early in the Bible (Gen. 35:17), and it comes to the fore in a political context in Exodus 1. The setting is in Egypt where the Hebrew people are mercilessly enslaved, forced to build the cities of Pithom and Rameses. But "the more they were oppressed, the more they multiplied and spread, so that the Egyptians came to dread the Israelites" (Exod. 1:12).

Against that background, we read an amazing story:

> The king of Egypt said to the Hebrew midwives, one of whom was named Shiphrah and the other Puah, "When you act as midwives to the Hebrew women, and see them on the birthstool, if it is a boy, kill him; but if it is a girl, she shall live." But the midwives feared God; they did not do as the king of Egypt commanded them, but they let the boys live. So the king of Egypt summoned the midwives and said to them, "Why have you done this, and allowed the boys to live?" The midwives said to Pharaoh, "Because the Hebrew women are not like the Egyptian women; for they are vigorous and give birth before the midwife comes to them." So God dealt well with the midwives; and the people multiplied and became very strong. And because the midwives feared God, he gave them families. (Exod. 1:15–21)

In *Bible Lives*, Jonathan Magonet has called these two midwives "the earliest and in some ways the most powerful examples of resistance to an evil regime." Ordered to perpetrate genocide, these two brave women risked their lives when they refused to obey the king's command. And while Shiphrah and Puah are not household names, they are outstanding examples of the courage that came from their faith in the Lord. Because they believed in the Lord God, they were *ezer* women, helping those who needed their help. Willing to stand bravely against evil, they used their professional expertise to aid their people in a time of crisis.

Sometimes, *ezer* women are called to stand against a powerful evil. Other times, *ezer* women are called to come alongside and help those who are weaker. This is as true today as it was thirty-four hundred years ago for Shiphrah and Puah. Both men and women have been created in God's image as "angled mirrors" to reflect who God is to people around them. Whether in the workplace or elsewhere, what could that look like for all of us today?

 Food for Thought

Have you faced situations at work where practices were contrary to God's purposes? If so, how have you handled them?

_____

_____

_____

_____

_____

_____

_____

On the whole, men and women are more alike than they are different, but women are created with enough differences from men that they bring unique gifts to the workplace. What gifts do you see either in yourself as an *ezer* woman, or in the *ezer* women around you in your workplace?

_____

_____

_____

_____

_____

_____

_____

Lesson #3: Miriam the *Ezer* Sister/Prophet (Exodus 2:1–10; 15:20)

When Shiphrah and Puah defied Pharaoh's order that they kill all Hebrew boy babies, these two midwives let the boys live because "they feared the Lord" (Exod. 1:17, 21). To "fear the Lord" means that we *reverence, honor,* or *stand in awe* of God. The Hebrew midwives believed that the Lord (*Yahweh*) stood against the gods of the Egyptians, and they honored him by saving the Hebrew boys. "Then Pharaoh commanded all his people, 'Every boy that is born to the Hebrews you shall throw into the Nile, but you shall let every girl live'" (Exod. 1:22).

Immediately after, we read about one of the Hebrew babies who were saved—Moses (Exod. 2:2–10). His mother hid him as long as possible, and then placed him in God's keeping in a basket floating on the Nile River. There, Pharaoh's daughter found and adopted the child, calling him "Moses" because she "drew him out of the water."

Are you struck with the irony of this situation? A Hebrew boy baby whom Pharaoh wanted killed at birth was adopted by Pharaoh's daughter and brought to live in the palace. In this, God honored the faith of the *ezer* midwives who did not kill the Hebrew boys at birth. But God also honored the courage and determination of Moses' *ezer* mother, Jochebed, and *ezer* sister, Miriam. Both Jochebed and Miriam took risks in placing Moses where Pharaoh's daughter would bathe. The king's decree was that the baby should be thrown into the Nile to die. Would Pharaoh's daughter comply with the king's command?

God honored the faith of four women: Shiphrah, Puah, Jochebed, and Miriam. Contrary to the king's command, the princess pitied the baby and provided for his welfare so she could adopt him as her own son. But also note Miriam's quick thinking when she immediately offered to find a Hebrew nurse for the discovered baby. This is part of being an *ezer* woman. God moved the Egyptian princess's heart to agree, so Moses' mother could nurse her baby openly—and was even paid by the princess for doing so!

Fast-forward many years. Moses grows up in the king's palace, but he eventually has to flee from Egypt after killing an Egyptian for beating a Hebrew slave. He settles in the land of Midian, marries, and works as a shepherd. There God calls him to return to Egypt and lead the Hebrew people out of bondage. You'll find the story of the Hebrew people's deliverance from the Egyptian king in Exodus 2–14. When the people are safe on the east side of the Red Sea, we once again meet Miriam (Exod. 15:20–21):

Then the prophet Miriam, Aaron's sister, took a tambourine in her hand; and all the women went out after her with tambourines and with dancing. And Miriam sang to them:

"Sing to the LORD, for he has triumphed gloriously; horse and rider he has thrown into the sea."

Miriam the *prophet*? Yes! This was part of Miriam's calling as a member of God's leadership team for the Hebrew people. The prophet Micah confirmed her role: "I brought you up from the land of Egypt, and redeemed you from the house of slavery; and I sent before you Moses, Aaron, and Miriam" (Mic. 6:4). Together two brothers and a sister were called by God to lead the Hebrew people into the Promised Land. While Miriam didn't always live up to her calling (see Num. 12), she was an *ezer* woman through and through. She came alongside those who needed her help throughout her long life.

Like Miriam, other women have gifts of all kinds and need to use them wherever they are—as the *ezer* women God created them to be.

 Food for Thought

If you are a woman, how do you feel about the gifts God has given you? If you are a man, how do you feel about the gifts of women in your workplace?

_____

_____

_____

_____

_____

If a woman understands herself as one created to be an *ezer*, what might that mean for the use of her gifts where she lives and works?

_____

_____

_____

_____

_____

_____

_____

Prayer

Lord,

Like Shiphrah and Puah, we want to honor you in what we do. And like Miriam, we want to use the gifts you've given us. Help us to grasp what that means today in every area of our lives.

Amen.

Chapter 3

Rahab

Lesson #1: Rahab the *Ezer* Protector (Joshua 2:1–24)

Sometimes God calls us to take a stand against our own culture because we've come to believe that it stands against what we know about God. We may face these kinds of decisions in the workplace. But once in a while, an event happens that changes the whole direction of our lives. That happened to a woman named Rahab more than three thousand years ago. She was a Canaanite (pagan) prostitute (or innkeeper, according to some scholars) who turned out to be God's *ezer* woman in the Hebrew people's time of need.

The Israelites had escaped from slavery in Egypt and eventually made their way to the east side of the Promised Land, Canaan. But that part of Canaan was well fortified, so Joshua (their leader) sent two spies to the first Canaanite city, Jericho, to learn what they could before preparing to attack. We find their story in Joshua 2:

> So [the spies] went, and entered the house of a prostitute whose name was Rahab, and spent the night there. The king of Jericho was told, "Some Israelites have come here tonight to search out the land." Then the king of Jericho sent orders to Rahab, "Bring out the men who have come to you, who entered your house, for they have come only to search out the whole land." But the woman took the two men and hid them. Then she said, "True, the men came to me, but I did not know where they came from. And when it was time to close the gate at dark, the men went out. Where the men went I do not know. Pursue them quickly, for you can overtake them." She had, however, brought them up to the roof

and hidden them with the stalks of flax that she had laid out on
the roof. So the men pursued them on the way to the Jordan as far
as the fords. As soon as the pursuers had gone out, the gate was
shut. (Josh. 2:1–7)

How is it that a pagan Canaanite, prostitute, and liar could pos-
sibly be an *ezer* woman? The answer lies in an amazing conversation she had with the two spies on the roof of her house. Observe
part of that conversation as Rahab speaks:

> "I know that the LORD has given you the land, and that dread of
> you has fallen on us, and that all the inhabitants of the land melt
> in fear before you. For we have heard how the LORD dried up the
> water of the Red Sea before you when you came out of Egypt, and
> what you did to the two kings of the Amorites that were beyond
> the Jordan, to Sihon and Og, whom you utterly destroyed. As soon
> as we heard it, our hearts melted, and there was no courage left
> in any of us because of you. The LORD your God is indeed God in
> heaven above and on earth below. Now then, since I have dealt
> kindly with you, swear to me by the LORD that you in turn will deal
> kindly with my family." (Josh. 2:8–12)

Rahab had come to believe that the Hebrews' Lord "is indeed
God in heaven above and on earth below." This understanding of
God, in contrast to the various gods of the Canaanites, brought
her to a new allegiance and willingness to shelter the spies. She
had become a believer in the Lord, and she was willing to risk her
life to further God's purposes.

Like Rahab, we may experience a major shift in our beliefs and
loyalties that completely changes our actions. Something in the
workplace forces our hand, and we have to make a decision to go
with what we believe about God at work in our world. At those mo-
ments we may be called to stand up against evil actions we earlier
would have ignored or even applauded. If we are called to stand for
God's purposes against the pressures of an ungodly society around
us, may God grant us the wisdom and courage to do just that.

 *Food for Thought*

How would you explain God's choice of Rahab as a key to Israel's victory over Jericho?

_____

_____

_____

_____

_____

_____

_____

What does it take to stand against evil actions that we earlier might have ignored or applauded?

_____

_____

_____

_____

_____

_____

_____

_____

Lesson #2: Impregnable Jericho Falls (Joshua 6:1–5)

Put yourself in Rahab's shoes. She risked her life by saving the lives of the two Hebrew spies. She followed their orders about gathering her family into her home on the wall. She hung the red cord in the window. Then she waited. And waited. And waited.

Thirty-four hundred years ago she had no cell phone to keep in touch with the two spies. She had no way of knowing why weeks went by with no sign of an approaching Hebrew army. She could not know that the Hebrews encamped on the east side of the Jordan River had to circumcise all the males before they could enter the Promised Land. Some scholars think that the invading Hebrew people now numbered more than two million. How many males had to be circumcised and then allowed to heal before they could pick up a sword and fight?

Then there was the Jordan River in full flood stage. How could so many people cross a raging river? For weeks Rahab must have glanced out her window daily, hoping to see the cloud of dust raised by an approaching army. Finally one day she did see them off in the distance. But as they drew closer, she was puzzled by what she saw. We read God's strange battle plan in Joshua 6:1–5:

> Now Jericho was shut up inside and out because of the Israelites; no one came out and no one went in. The LORD said to Joshua, "See, I have handed Jericho over to you, along with its king and soldiers. You shall march around the city, all the warriors circling the city once. Thus you shall do for six days, with seven priests bearing seven trumpets of rams' horns before the ark. On the seventh day you shall march around the city seven times, the priests blowing the trumpets. When they make a long blast with the ram's horn, as soon as you hear the sound of the trumpet, then all the people shall shout with a great shout; and the wall of the city will fall down flat, and all the people shall charge straight ahead."

What kind of battle plan is that? Could anything be less likely to succeed? Can you imagine Rahab's astonishment when on the seventh day the Israelites gave that great shout and all around her the walls of the city fell inward so that the soldiers could climb over the rubble and engage the enemy?

In her conversation with the two spies, Rahab had declared that Israel's God was indeed "God in heaven above and on earth below." Now she witnessed the power of that God for whom she had risked her life.

Sometimes in life we wait and wait and wait for God to act. But Rahab's God is also our God who will in power—and sometimes by very unusual circumstances—come to our aid. From Rahab we learn that God will accomplish his purposes in his own time. Our task is to put our trust in him.

 Food for Thought

Sometimes in the Bible we see God act in ways that seem improbable at best, or even silly. Why might God choose to act in such ways?

_____

_____

_____

_____

_____

_____

How does that experience impact our trust in him?

_____

_____

_____

_____

_____

_____

_____

_____

Lesson #3: Pagan Rahab Becomes One with the People of God (Joshua 6:22–25)

Can you imagine Rahab's thoughts as she stared out her window at the total destruction of her city? Would Israel's God come through for her, or would she perish in all of the carnage? We find the answer in Joshua 6:22–23:

> Joshua said to the two men who had spied out the land, "Go into the prostitute's house, and bring the woman out of it and all who belong to her, as you swore to her." So the young men who had been spies went in and brought Rahab out, along with her father, her mother, her brothers and all who belonged to her—they brought all her kindred out—and set them outside the camp of Israel.

Safe! Rahab had bet on Israel's God, and she and all of her family were saved. But there is more to the story: "Rahab the prostitute, with her family and all who belonged to her, Joshua spared. Her family has lived in Israel ever since. For she hid the messengers whom Joshua sent to spy out Jericho" (Josh. 6:25).

Rahab was now one with God's people. The fact that she had been a pagan prostitute was irrelevant. Sometimes we may think that justice is served only if people pay for their sins. But God thinks differently. The Apostle Paul describes God's approach in these words: "For by grace you have been saved through faith, and this is not your own doing; it is the gift of God—not the result of works, so that no one may boast" (Eph. 2:8–9). Rahab had placed her faith in Israel's God and that was enough.

It is the same for us. Whatever we've done in the past becomes irrelevant when by faith we are washed clean by God's act of unmerited favor. God gives us a new beginning. What matters is what we do with the life God is giving us.

For some Christians it would already be a stretch that Rahab was allowed to become one with God's people in Israel. But the story is even more amazing. It turns out that Rahab's name comes up in unexpected places in the New Testament. In Matthew 1:5–6 we read, "Salmon the father of Boaz by Rahab, and Boaz the father of Obed by Ruth, and Obed the father of Jesse, and Jesse the father of King David." Not only was Rahab a part of Israel, but she was an ancestor of Israel's greatest king, David. And not only that: if you read the rest of Matthew's genealogy, you discover that she is in the lineage of Jesus, the Savior of the world. God didn't hold her accountable for her past. He looked at what she could become.

Rahab stands before us, witnessing to the possibilities within each of us. Wherever you are, whatever may haunt you from your past, know that God looks, not at that, but at what you can become by faith.

Food for Thought

How does Rahab's story help us understand God's grace, a grace that is greater than all our sins?

_____

_____

_____

_____

_____

_____

_____

How might we reflect God's grace toward others in our workplace?

_____

_____

_____

_____

_____

_____

_____

_____

Prayer

Lord, I need to know that you are with me when I face issues in my work world that are contrary to your kingdom values. Strengthen my backbone and give me courage to reflect your values where needed.

Amen.

Chapter 4

Deborah

Lesson #1: Deborah the *Ezer* Leader/Judge (Judges 4:4–5)

To this point, we've looked at *ezer* women who came alongside those who needed their help in the midst of their daily responsibilities—midwives, a mother and daughter team, a foreigner, and even a Jericho prostitute. But sometimes God calls a woman to the highest level of leadership in a crisis moment.

This happened to the woman Deborah, wife of Lappidoth. She had gifts for leadership, and was both a prophet and a wise woman who "was judging Israel. She used to sit under the palm of Deborah between Ramah and Bethel in the hill country of Ephraim; and the Israelites came up to her for judgment" (Judg. 4:4–5). What did that mean? According to Exodus 18:25–26, "Moses chose able men from all Israel and appointed them as heads over the people . . . and they judged the people at all times." Here is a woman in that position.

The book of Judges reveals a troubled and difficult three-century era in the life of Israel. The strong leaders Moses and Joshua had passed away, and the judges who followed them were primarily military leaders who rose to power in times of national crisis. And what caused these crises? Attracted by their neighbors' pagan practices, the Israelites often strayed from faith in the Lord God. Human sacrifice, ritual prostitution, and other practices replaced the worship of Israel's God. When various tribes of Israelites shifted into these vile practices, God allowed neighboring nations to conquer them. Sometimes this meant being enslaved; other times it meant having to pay exorbitant tributes. Sooner or later, someone would call out to the Lord God for deliverance. A judge would come to the fore and organize a military campaign to throw off the oppressor. Then the tribe would live in peace until the next apostasy from faith and trust in God.

Some judges were better than others, and in Judges 4 we meet Deborah, who combined the best qualities of a worthy judge: she ably settled people's disputes, and she was also a brilliant military strategist when needed. But the first characteristic mentioned in Judges 4:4 is that she was a prophet. Centuries earlier under Moses' leadership, God called priests to teach the law to the people. When the priests failed to do so, God raised up prophets to bring the people back to faith in the Lord. That was Deborah's task as judge over Israel.

And what was the situation in Israel when she came into that office? Judges 4:1–3 gives us the situation Deborah faced as judge:

> The Israelites again did what was evil in the sight of the LORD, after Ehud [the judge] died. So the LORD sold them into the hand of King Jabin of Canaan, who reigned in Hazor; the commander of his army was Sisera, who lived in Harosheth-ha-goiim. Then the Israelites cried out to the LORD for help; for he had nine hundred chariots of iron, and had oppressed the Israelites cruelly twenty years.

Deborah stepped into leadership in Israel at a time of crisis. She could do so because she was also God's prophet, one who knew God and was prepared to represent him truly as God's "angled mirror" in a time of apostasy.

Food for Thought

Deborah's workplace was a spot under her palm tree between Ramah and Bethel where the people came to have her judge their issues. Describe your workplace.

_____

_____

_____

_____

_____

_____

_____

If a crisis arises in your workplace, who steps in to address it and what values does that person bring to the situation?

_____

_____

_____

_____

_____

_____

_____

Lesson #2: Deborah Leads Her People to Freedom (Judges 4:6–16)

Think about the geography of Israel: Deborah led the nation from "the *hill country* of Ephraim." King Jabin's power lay in his nine hundred chariots of iron, but the king's heavy chariots could operate only on flat land, not in the mountainous south. Because much of the land of Israel was mountainous (and thus untouched by King Jabin's army), Deborah could have ignored the plight of those in the flat northern territory. But she did not. An *ezer* woman who has the ability to come to the aid of the helpless accepts the challenge to do so:

> She sent and summoned Barak son of Abinoam from Kedesh in Naphtali, and said to him, "The LORD, the God of Israel, commands you, 'Go, take position at Mount Tabor, bringing ten thousand from the tribe of Naphtali and the tribe of Zebulun. I will draw out Sisera, the general of Jabin's army, to meet you by the Wadi Kishon with his chariots and his troops; and I will give him into your hand.'" Barak said to her, "If you will go with me, I will go; but if you will not go with me, I will not go." And she said, "I will surely go with you; nevertheless, the road on which you are going will not lead to your glory; for the LORD will sell Sisera into the hand of a woman." Then Deborah got up and went with Barak to Kedesh. (Judg. 4:6–9)

Barak's ragtag army of ill-equipped men on the slopes of Mount Tabor may have felt hopeless as they looked at Sisera's far more powerful army spread out on the plain below them. But Deborah stood next to Barak, and at the right moment she shouted, "Up! For this is the day in which the LORD has given Sisera into your hand. The LORD is indeed going out before you" (Judg. 4:14). And as Barak's army moved down the mountain slopes, "the LORD threw Sisera and all his chariots and all his army into a panic before Barak; Sisera got down from his chariot and fled away on foot, while Barak pursued the chariots and the army to Haro-sheth-ha-goiim. All the army of Sisera fell by the sword; no one was left" (Judg. 4:15–16). God turned the tide of battle for the Israelites. (For Sisera's dramatic demise by the hand of another woman, Jael, read Judges 4:17–22.)

Judges 4 ends by telling us that "on that day God subdued King Jabin of Canaan before the Israelites" (v. 23). The woman Deborah, gifted by God, had been willing to lead in a time of crisis, and God gave victory to a ragtag, poorly equipped army. Clearly, it was *God* who brought about the rout of Sisera's army.

Consider that we may be called to step up and lead in times of crisis. Do we have Deborah's confidence in God to do this?

 Food for Thought

What part do you think Deborah's faith in God played in the use of her gifts?

_____

_____

_____

_____

_____

_____

_____

What part do you think your faith in God should play in the use
of your gifts?

_____

_____

_____

_____

_____

_____

_____

Lesson #3: Deborah's Source of Power (Judges 5)

How did God pull off such a resounding victory? When Deborah
and Barak later sang their victory song (Judg. 5), we learn the
answer to that question.

> "LORD, when you went out . . . the earth trembled, and the heavens
> poured, the clouds indeed poured water. . . . The stars fought from
> heaven, from their courses they fought against Sisera. The torrent
> Kishon swept them away, the onrushing torrent, the torrent
> Kishon." (Judg. 5:4, 20–21)

The historian Josephus tells us that as Sisera and his army ad-
vanced east to meet Barak's army, a sleet storm hit the Canaanite
army full in the face, blinding the archers, the chariot drivers,
and their horses. Whether Sisera faced sleet or heavy rain, the
three-point consequence was the same: both men and beasts were
blinded; the rain soon turned the plain into a muddy swamp, trap-

ping the wheels of the iron chariots sinking into it; and the brook Kishon, normally no more than a trickling stream, overflowed its banks and flooded the land, carrying warriors out to sea in its turbulent waters. Witnessing God's deliverance, Deborah and Barak sang their praise to God: "March on, my soul, with might!" (Judg. 5:21). God was their might, their help.

In the book of Judges, Deborah is the model leader, equal to the greatest leaders of Israel. No other judge is called a prophet (Judg. 4:4), which indicates how closely she resembles Moses and Joshua, to whom God also spoke directly.

What does it take for an *ezer* woman to step forward and lead? Did you note how often Deborah spoke from her confidence that it was the Lord, Israel's God, who would overcome the enemy? This was the prophet speaking. Undergirding her gifts and her influence was her unshakeable faith in God, which gave her the strength to lead her people. But she also had to remind herself that God's victory over King Jabin and his general Sisera was not the end of her career. We hear that in her words, "March on, my soul, with might!" Keep moving. Don't rest on the laurels of victory. God has much more that needs to be done to counteract the evil in this world.

Not every man or woman is called to lead, but every woman is created by God to be an *ezer*, to come alongside those who are helpless without her aid. Like Deborah, our confidence is in God, not in ourselves. And we remind ourselves to "march on with might" because we do so in the strength of the Lord our God.

 *Food for Thought*

Why do you think Deborah, after that stunning victory over superior military might, had to remind herself to "march on with might"?

_____

_____

_____

_____

_____

_____

While you may not have Deborah's gifts or calling, what can you learn from her that will help you reflect God's image and God's will to people around you?

_____

_____

_____

_____

_____

_____

_____

Prayer

Lord,

Give us courage to reflect your values where needed. Help us also to see how Deborah's story can encourage us in our work today. In whatever challenges we face, help us to practice her confidence in you.

Amen.

Chapter 5

Ruth

Lesson #1: Ruth the *Ezer* Daughter-in-Law (Ruth 1)

One of the difficult situations in life comes when we find ourselves as "outliers," someone outside the "in-group." Sometimes this happens because we march to a different drumbeat—that is, we're just different in the way we act or speak. Other times, it's a function of our gender, our ethnicity, or our lack of educational or economic privilege. But in any case, we must deal with the reality in life that we sometimes find ourselves outside the inner circle. How do we cope with that?

It's easy to disconnect that reality from our faith in God and the fact that God is with us even in our outsider situation. But we can draw courage from the example of another *ezer* woman we meet in the Old Testament. Ruth is a Moabite, part of a tribal group hated by Israelites. As long as she remained in Moab, she was part of that in-group. But when she made a decision that took her to Israel, she became an outsider and would have to deal with all of the disadvantages of her ethnic identity in a foreign land.

The backstory is this: The town of Bethlehem faced a prolonged famine, and an Israelite family headed by Elimelech decided to move to Moab where food was available. Once there, they settled down and his two sons eventually married Moabite women, Ruth and Orpah. Then tragedy struck and both the father and the two sons died, leaving three widows. The mother, Naomi, counseled her two daughters-in-law to return to their Moabite families where new marriages might be arranged for them. Orpah chose to do so, but Ruth refused to leave Naomi. Instead, in Ruth 1:16–17, she speaks some familiar words to her mother-in-law, words we often hear at weddings and on other occasions:

"Do not press me to leave you
    or to turn back from following you!
Where you go, I will go;
    where you lodge, I will lodge;
your people shall be my people,
    and your God my God.
Where you die, I will die—
    there will I be buried.
May the LORD do thus and so to me,
    and more as well,
if even death parts me from you!"

These are the words of an *ezer* woman. Putting aside her own interests, Ruth knew that Naomi would need her support as they adjusted to life in Bethlehem. But she also embraced Naomi's God as well as her homeland. So together they journeyed to an unknown future, trekking from Moab to Bethlehem in Israel.

When the two women arrived in Bethlehem, Naomi's friends could scarcely recognize her. In her grief, Naomi told them, "Call me no longer 'Naomi.' Call me 'Mara,' for the Almighty has dealt bitterly with me. I went away full, but the LORD has brought me back empty" (Ruth 1:20–21). Obviously, Ruth would have to be strong for the two of them. Outsider or not, her work was cut out for her.

Food for Thought

Situations can arise in our workplace that require us to be strong for others. How can Ruth's example encourage us in that task?

_____

_____

_____

_____

_____

_____

The position of "outsider" is rarely comfortable, but in what ways can it open doors to ministry for us in our workplace?

_____

_____

_____

_____

_____

_____

Lesson #2: Ruth the *Ezer* Provider (Ruth 2)

Arriving back in Bethlehem with nothing but the neglected land belonging to Naomi's deceased husband, Elimelech, Ruth stepped up to the task of providing for her mother-in-law. Ruth received permission to glean in various fields, retrieving grains of barley the reapers left behind. One field belonged to a wealthy landowner named Boaz (Naomi's distant relative) who took an interest in this determined young woman.

Imagine Ruth on hands and knees, following the reapers as she gathered kernels of grain they had left behind. How much could she find to feed herself and her mother-in-law between now and the next harvest? Diligently she kept at her task, so much so that when the landowner, Boaz, asked the reapers' supervisor about her, he praised her determination not to rest or to miss any barley on the ground (Ruth 2:5–7). Impressed, Boaz invited Ruth to glean only in his fields and also offered her protection from any predatory men in the area.

Boaz played a key role in his treatment of this alien woman in his workplace, ordering his own men not to touch Ruth (Ruth 2:9). Through his actions, he showed his willingness to stand up for a vulnerable worker. This may well be the world's earliest recorded anti-sexual harassment policy in the workplace.

Think about Ruth's decision to care for her widowed mother-in-law, even when it meant becoming a hated foreigner in a new land. Why would she forfeit the possibility of a new marriage in her own land to one of her own people? What drove her decision to stay with Naomi? Note her words to her mother-in-law: not only would Naomi's people become her people, but Naomi's God would become her God. Born and reared in a land worshiping Moabite gods, Ruth had come to believe (like Rahab before her) that Israel's God is "God in heaven above and on earth below."

This new allegiance enabled her to make a decision that went against the advice of her mother-in-law. She had begun to march to a different drumbeat, and her ethnic identity became secondary to her faith in the Lord God. In this Moabite woman, we see the quality of *ezer* in her loyalty to her mother-in-law and her willingness to work hard to support them both.

Many factors beyond our control can contribute to an outsider reality. If we find ourselves in such a situation, we can learn from Ruth that what matters is less the way we're treated and more how God will use us in that situation. That means that we sometimes opt for the hard road "to Bethlehem" as an outsider, because there are people who need the help we can give them.

 Food for Thought

As you think about Ruth's decision to leave her homeland and deliberately become an outsider in Israel for her mother-in-law's benefit, what do you think motivated her?

_____

_____

_____

_____

_____

_____

Boaz ensured that his women workers were treated with respect, but that wasn't true everywhere in Israel—especially during the notoriously dark times of the judges. How is your work environment regarding harassment of any kind? Is anyone being treated disrespectfully? If so, what can you do about it?

_____

_____

_____

_____

_____

_____

_____

_____

Lesson #3: God Blesses Ruth's *Ezer* Grit (Ruth 3–4)

Ruth 2 ends with these words: "She stayed close to the young women of Boaz, gleaning until the end of the barley and wheat harvests; and she lived with her mother-in-law." But that's not the end of this fascinating story. Naomi took a long-shot gamble with her daughter-in-law's life and reputation as she plotted how Ruth could propose marriage to Boaz, the field's owner. Read Ruth 3 for the details of this daring plot!

Knowing that Boaz would be winnowing barley at the threshing floor that night, Naomi instructed Ruth:

> "Now wash and anoint yourself, and put on your best clothes and go down to the threshing floor; but do not make yourself known to the man until he has finished eating and drinking. When he lies down, observe the place where he lies; then, go and uncover his feet and lie down; and he will tell you what to do." (Ruth 3:3–4)

Ruth followed orders, and at midnight Boaz was startled to discover a woman lying at his feet. When he asked who she was, she replied, "I am Ruth, your servant; spread your cloak over your servant, for you are next-of-kin" (3:9). What was this "spread your cloak over me" about? In the ancient Middle East, it was tantamount to a proposal of marriage. And what was this "next-of-kin" about? In that culture, when a woman was widowed, the next brother of her deceased husband was legally obliged to marry her and raise up children to continue the deceased brother's line. What sounds like an outlandish statement on Ruth's part to Boaz was actually fully understandable in that culture.

And how did Boaz respond?

> "May you be blessed by the LORD, my daughter; this last instance of your loyalty [to Naomi] is better than the first. . . . And now, my daughter, do not be afraid, I will do for you all that you ask, for all the assembly of my people know that you are a worthy woman. But now, though it is true that I am a near kinsman, there is another kinsman more closely related than I." (Ruth 3:10–12)

Ruth's proposal was accepted, but there was a hitch: someone else had a prior claim that could lead to owning Naomi's land.

Now read Ruth 4. Boaz was able to "close the deal" by reminding the nearer kinsman that while getting Naomi's land was part of the bargain, it also included marrying Ruth. Any children born to them would maintain "the dead man's name on his inheritance" (Ruth 4:5). When the nearer kinsman backed out of the deal, Boaz promptly married Ruth. When she later gave birth to a son, he became Naomi's grandson to carry on the family name.

It's a lovely story, and it turns out that Ruth and Boaz were the great-grandparents of Israel's greatest king, David. The outsider was now part of God's people in Bethlehem, and God had chosen that she (like Rahab) should be an ancestor not only of King David but also of the King of kings, Jesus Christ (Matt. 1:5).

Food for Thought

God rewarded outsider Ruth's decision with inclusion in Israel's royal history. Can you see ways in which God could use your "outsider" position?

_____

_____

_____

_____

_____

_____

You may be an "outsider" as a Christian in a secular workplace. Mirroring Ruth's work, what God-honoring strategies could you use to bring blessing to others?

_____

_____

_____

_____

_____

_____

Prayer

Lord,

We see that you can use us in important ways if we're willing to be "outsiders" with a mission. But it's not easy. Help us to believe that you are with us wherever we go and that you will work through us in ways that may exceed our wildest imaginations.

Amen.

Chapter 6

Abigail

Lesson #1: Abigail in a Miserable Marriage (1 Samuel 25:2–3)

In order to head off disaster, when is it right to go up against those who have power over us? To get at that, we turn to another *ezer* woman in the Old Testament. This story is about a wealthy rancher, Nabal, who had huge holdings (three thousand sheep and one thousand goats), requiring others to care for and protect these animals in the highlands of Judah. The Bible tells us that he also had a clever and beautiful wife, Abigail, but that he himself was surly and mean. (His Hebrew name actually means "foolish" or "wicked." The force of the Hebrew was that he was harsh and overbearing.)

At that time, David and his band of followers were being chased all over the southern wilderness of Israel by King Saul, who was determined to kill David (1 Sam. 23:15–24:22). How could the fugitives survive? Where could such a large band of men find food? To support themselves, David and his men gave protection to Nabal's shepherds throughout the year, and expected that Nabal would reward them with food at sheep-shearing time.

Anticipating some payment for services rendered during the year, David sent ten of his men to Nabal, who were to tell Nabal from David,

> "Peace be to you, and peace be to your house, and peace be to all that you have. I hear that you have shearers [the time for reward]; now your shepherds have been with us, and we did them no harm,

and they missed nothing, all the time they were in Carmel. Ask
your young men, and they will tell you. Therefore let my young
men find favor in your sight; for we have come on a feast day.
Please give whatever you have at hand to your servants and to
your son David." (1 Sam. 25:6–8)

It seemed like a reasonable request, but the rich rancher replied:

"Who is David? Who is the son of Jesse? . . . Shall I take my bread
and my water and the meat that I have butchered for my shear-
ers, and give it to men who come from I do not know where?"
(1 Sam. 25:10–11)

When David's men returned empty-handed, their leader responded:
"Every man strap on his sword!" and about four hundred men set
out with David (leaving two hundred behind to guard their belong-
ings). Their goal was to wipe out Nabal and his entire household.

Meanwhile one of the shepherds told Abigail:

"[David's] men were very good to us, and we suffered no harm,
and we never missed anything when we were in the fields, as long
as we were with them; they were a wall to us both by night and
by day, all the while we were with them keeping the sheep. Now
therefore know this and consider what you should do; for evil has
been decided against our master and against all his house; he is so
ill-natured that no one can speak to him." (1 Sam. 25:15–17)

In the patriarchal society of the ancient Near East, Abigail would
not ordinarily do anything contrary to her husband's actions or
strictures. But the lives of her entire household were at stake!
What should she do?

Perhaps you've found yourself in a similar situation where you
were faced with a completely unreasonable but powerful person
in the workplace. Caution may have told you to put up with the
situation, but you and others could be endangered by this person's actions.

 *Food for Thought*

How much are you willing to risk in order to change a bad situation?

_____

_____

_____

_____

_____

_____

_____

When an employer denies compensation to an employee, what recourse might be possible to redress the situation?

_____

_____

_____

_____

_____

_____

_____

Lesson #2: *Ezer* Abigail Meets the Challenge (1 Samuel 25:18–35)

When nasty people rise to power in the workplace, how can we deal with them? For Abigail, saving the lives of everyone in her household became the priority. To do that, she had to take two major risks. The first risk was to ignore Nabal's decision by calling for several donkeys and large amounts of food that she would personally take to David, hoping to head off his attack. In 1 Samuel 25:18–23, we watch her pack up two hundred loaves of bread, two skins of wine, five dressed sheep, five measures of roasted grain, one hundred clusters of raisins, and two hundred cakes of figs. Would she be able to do this without Nabal's knowledge?

When the donkeys were packed, she mounted another donkey and began the trek to meet an angry man with four hundred armed warriors. This was the second risk. Would David strike her down or would he receive her gift? He had already sworn to his men that he would leave no one alive at Nabal's ranch. David was out for blood. Meeting him on the road, she fell on her face to the ground before him, pleading with him to accept the gift she had brought. It was a long speech (1 Sam. 25:24–31), but it was effective.

When David heard her plea, he responded:

> "Blessed be the LORD, the God of Israel, who sent you to meet me today! Blessed be your good sense, and blessed be you, who have kept me today from bloodguilt and from avenging myself by my own hand! For as surely as the LORD the God of Israel lives, who has restrained me from hurting you, unless you had hurried and come to meet me, truly by morning there would not have been left to Nabal so much as one male. . . . Go up to your house in peace; see, I have heeded your voice, and I have granted your petition."
> (1 Sam. 25:32–35)

Notice how David interpreted Abigail's action. He blessed her for three reasons: He recognized that (1) *God* had sent her to intercept him; (2) her action showed her good sense; and (3) by her action she kept David from bloodguilt and an act of revenge. David saw the hand of the Lord in her action. Abigail was God's messenger to him, and he took note of her "good sense." So a sensible *ezer* woman in God's hand kept David from a terrible deed.

Abigail had headed off one disaster, but once David's wrath was appeased and he turned back, she had to return to her house. She would have to face her husband, knowing full well how he would react to what she had done. Arriving back home, she saw that Nabal was drunk after a large feast, so she said nothing to him until the next morning. But when he had sobered up, she told him what had happened. When he heard what might have been, "his heart died within him; he became like a stone. About ten days later the LORD struck Nabal, and he died" (1 Sam. 25:37–38).

When we take risks for just and honorable reasons, we rarely know ahead of time how it will turn out. Abigail could have no certainty about David's reaction to her, or how Nabal would act after learning the truth about his rash refusal to honor the work of David's men on his behalf. A risk is just that—a *risk* with the possibility of failure. But in Abigail's speech to David, she was clear that "the LORD will certainly make my lord a sure house, because my lord is fighting the battles of the LORD" (1 Sam. 25:28). She had confidence that God was involved, and she could trust him as she stepped out of her culturally subordinate role in a righteous cause.

Food for Thought

Has there ever been a situation at your workplace where you needed to say or do something to avoid a major problem? Describe what happened.

_____

_____

_____

_____

_____

_____

_____

In what ways will your faith direct your response to evil situations in the workplace?

_____

_____

_____

_____

_____

_____

_____

Lesson #3: *Ezer* Abigail Marries David (1 Samuel 25:39–44)

Nabal's death was not the end of Abigail's story.

> When David heard that Nabal was dead, he said, "Blessed be the
> LORD who has judged the case of Nabal's insult to me, and has kept
> back his servant from evil; the LORD has returned the evildoing of
> Nabal upon his own head." Then David sent and wooed Abigail, to
> make her his wife. (1 Sam. 25:39)

A proposal of marriage from Israel's future king? Abigail said yes
and became David's wife. He knew a wise woman when he saw her!
This is not to say that Abigail's life would be one of perpetual hap-
piness. She was now married to a fugitive on the run from a jealous
king. And she had to contend with life as one wife among others
as David had already married Michal and Ahinoam. The fairy-tale
"happily ever after" rarely comes to many men or women in this life.

Although David was called "a man after God's own heart," he did
not always act honorably, and it later became necessary for the
prophet Nathan to confront him with his sins. Yet he also loved
God wholeheartedly, and in time he became Israel's greatest king.
But we cannot assume that Abigail's life as one of his eight wives
was easy.

When, like Abigail, we take bad matters in hand and work to
change them, we cannot know for certain that all will turn out
well. Sometimes we see decisions in the workplace that lead to
injustice for individuals or harm to the business. And when we
"blow the whistle," we may lose our job. Just as Abigail risked her
life to save lives, we may risk our livelihood if we intervene.

But that's where our confidence in God comes in. We know that
God loves justice and when we act justly, we are doing his will. If
we do his will, then we can trust his love and know he will bring
us through any consequences of our actions. As with Abigail, God
may send us into situations requiring this kind of risk. Once in

them, though, we are called to use good sense as we take actions that stave off disaster. At the same time, as "angled mirrors" we stand in God's stead in the workplace, reflecting holy, divine values through our actions. When we do that, we honor our God.

 Food for Thought

How would you feel if you were called to take a stand against evil that occurred in your workplace?

_____

_____

_____

_____

_____

_____

How does your confidence in God empower you to confront evil in a godly way?

_____

_____

_____

_____

_____

_____

Prayer

Lord,

I know that you led Abigail to do what she did. Help me also to know when you're leading me to confront evil if I see it in my workplace. Please enable me to see myself as an "angled mirror," reflecting your values where I work. Then give me the strength to do what you want done to confront this evil, while always being a light from your kingdom of justice and peace.

Amen.

Chapter 7

Huldah and Esther

Lesson #1: Huldah and Esther, *Ezer* Women in Crisis Times (2 Kings 22; Esther 1)

How do you react when something big interrupts the normal structure of your everyday life? Do new responsibilities make you anxious? Or are you usually excited about new possibilities?

Let's explore the experience of two women in the Old Testament whose placid lives were interrupted.

Huldah lived "in Jerusalem in the Second Quarter" (2 Kings 22:14), which was considered the "university" quarter. From that some rabbis have suggested that she was a teacher by profession. She was married to Shallum, the keeper of the sacred wardrobe for priests, who was also the uncle of the prophet Jeremiah (Jer. 32:7). Like Jeremiah, Huldah was a prophet. She could interpret God's word and will to the people. Esther lived with her cousin Mordecai as exiles in Persia.

The backstory for both of these women is one repeated again and again in the history of Israel. The Hebrew people were often bent toward forsaking the Lord God as they practiced the evil activities of neighboring countries and worshiped false gods. Many of Israel's and Judah's kings allowed practices such as ritual prostitution in the name of some god or sacrificing children in the fires of Moloch. God sent prophets to call the people back to righteous living, but the people had a curvature of the soul toward false gods.

Huldah lived in a time when a good king had finally come to Judah's throne after a series of evil kings had all but destroyed the nation religiously. Esther lived more than a century later, when God allowed these bent people to be taken into exile by Babylon for seventy years. Both women lived quiet lives until the moment when each was thrust on stage to carry out an important task.

In Huldah's story, young King Josiah instituted major reforms in the Hebrew nation of Judah. His grandfather, Manasseh (who ruled Judah for fifty-five years), had led his people "to do more evil than the nations had done that the LORD destroyed before the people of Israel" (2 Kings 21:9), and his father Amon was no better. Unlike them, however, Josiah "did what was right in the sight of the LORD, and . . . he did not turn aside to the right or to the left" (2 Kings 22:2).

Josiah began his reforms with God's temple, which was in need of major repairs. In the process, workers stumbled over an ancient manuscript, "the book of the law." When parts of the book were read to King Josiah, "he tore his clothes . . . saying . . . '[G]reat is the wrath of the LORD that is kindled against us, because our ancestors did not obey the words of this book'" (2 Kings 22:11–13). If this book meant what he thought it meant, then disaster loomed! He ordered his staff to find someone who could explain what he was hearing. Where was a prophet who could interpret this book accurately for the king, his courtiers, and the high priest?

Esther's story begins at an all-male banquet when the inebriated king Ahasuerus commands his servants to bring in Queen Vashti so he can show her off to his guests (Esth. 1:10–11). But Vashti, sensing the indignity of the request, refuses to come (Esth. 1:12). As a result, the men fear her example will encourage their wives likewise to stand up to them (Esth. 1:13–18). Vashti is subsequently removed from her position, and Ahasuerus begins the search for a new queen (Esth. 1:21–2:4). (Although the relationship between Vashti and Ahasuerus can be considered a family matter, every royal family has political ramifications. Vashti's situation is therefore a workplace issue, in which the boss attempts to exploit a woman because of her gender and then terminates her when she fails to comply. Unfortunately, as the writer of Ecclesiastes says, there is nothing new under the sun.)

In the process of this search, Esther is one of many beautiful women brought to the palace harem for a yearlong beauty treatment before being brought to the king. Her quiet life outside the palace is now gone because she is part of the emperor's harem. Esther's "gift" from God is not prophecy like Huldah's, but the gift of her beauty. Neither woman sought the gift that brought them to royal attention. But because they had the gift, they had a responsibility for it.

Gifts vary greatly, but whatever your gift may be, God has given it to you to be used, not to be put on a shelf somewhere. Your present work may not seem to tap into your gift, but at some point an occasion will arise requiring that you step up and use your gift for the benefit of God's people. Are you ready for that?

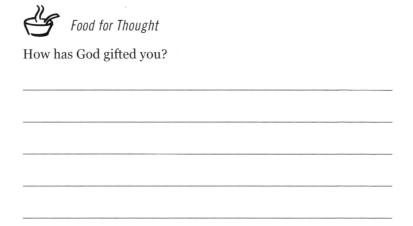

Food for Thought

How has God gifted you?

_____

_____

_____

_____

_____

_____

_____

_____

How are you stewarding that gift for God's kingdom purposes?

_____

_____

_____

_____

_____

_____

_____

Lesson #2: Huldah the *Ezer* Prophet (2 Kings 22:14–20)

The capital city of Jerusalem did not lack prophets when King Josiah sent his team to find one. "The word of the LORD that came to Zephaniah . . . in the days of King Josiah . . . of Judah" (Zeph. 1:1). Jeremiah also prophesied in Judah during Josiah's reign: "The words of Jeremiah . . . to whom the word of the LORD came in the days of King Josiah" (Jer. 1:1–2). Does it surprise you that the high priest and the king's secretary chose to ask a woman, Huldah, to interpret the book for them? Enter this truly *ezer* woman, coming to the aid of her king and nation.

What is striking in Huldah's approach is her straight-shooting interpretation of the book:

"Thus says the LORD, the God of Israel: Tell the man who sent you to me, Thus says the LORD, I will indeed bring disaster on this place and on its inhabitants—all the words of the book that the king of Judah has read. Because they have abandoned me and have made offerings to other gods, so that they have provoked me to anger with all the work of their hands, therefore my wrath will be kindled against this place, and it will not be quenched. But as to the king of Judah, who sent you to inquire of the LORD, thus shall you say to him, Thus says the LORD, the God of Israel: Regarding the words that you have heard, because your heart was penitent, and you humbled yourself before the LORD, when you heard how I spoke against this place, and against its inhabitants, that they should become a desolation and a curse, and because you have torn your clothes and wept before me, I also have heard you, says the LORD. Therefore, I will gather you to your ancestors, and you shall be gathered to your grave in peace; your eyes shall not see all the disaster that I will bring on this place." (2 Kings 22:15–20)

The high priest and the king's secretary took Huldah's prophecy back to King Josiah, who then instituted a massive purge of the idolatry and evil practices from Judah. Meanwhile, Huldah quietly returned to her duties at the university. Most of 2 Kings 23 details the extent of the king's reform. Taking Huldah's interpretation of God's word seriously,

The king stood in his place and made a covenant before the LORD, to follow the LORD, keeping his commandments, his decrees, and his statutes, with all his heart and all his soul, to perform the words of the covenant that were written in this book. Then he made all who were present in Jerusalem and in Benjamin pledge themselves to it. . . . Josiah took away all the abominations from all the territory that belonged to the people of Israel, and made all who were in Israel worship the LORD their God. All his days they did not turn away from following the LORD, the God of their ancestors. (2 Chron. 34:31–33)

God led the leaders of the nation to ask a woman to interpret the Scripture for the king. She was an *ezer* woman: she could tell them what they needed to hear, directly and without apology. In the best sense of the word, she became their helper, enabling them to understand the word of the Lord.

At times, women may find their work routine interrupted by a request to step into a different role, one that pushes them to speak for God in a public arena. Huldah's experience challenges women to accept these new opportunities or requests without shying away from them. In the process, they may discover that God has given them gifts beyond those they use every day.

 Food for Thought

How do you react when your schedule is interrupted with a request to do something quite different?

_____

_____

_____

_____

_____

_____

_____

When you're asked to do something culturally out of the ordinary (like Huldah interpreting the book for the king), what reasons might push you to say yes or no to the new assignment?

_____

_____

_____

_____

_____

_____

Lesson #3: Esther the *Ezer* Beauty (Esther 2–10)

Exploitation of women was evident in the ancient world, and the kingdom of Persia was no exception. When Ahasuerus deposed his queen, Vashti, the search continued for a replacement from his harem. After night visits to other women in the harem, "the king loved Esther more than all the other women; of all the virgins she won his favor and devotion, so that he set the royal crown on her head and made her queen instead of Vashti" (Esth. 2:17).

Meanwhile, another drama was unfolding outside the palace gate. Esther's cousin, Mordecai, learned of a plot to assassinate the king. He told Queen Esther, who then told the king, and the two would-be assassins were hanged. Ahasuerus owed his life to Mordecai. In a separate event, the king elevated the evil Haman to a top-ranking position in his government, requiring others to bow down in his presence. When Mordecai refused to do so, Haman was so incensed that he plotted "to destroy all the Jews, the people of Mordecai, throughout the whole kingdom" (Esth. 3:6). In exchange for a large sum of money to be paid into the king's treasury, Haman acquired an edict from Ahasuerus not only for Mordecai's death but for the death of all Jews in the empire.

Although Esther was sequestered in the palace, Mordecai sent word to her of the coming bloodbath and asked her to "go to the king to make supplication to him and entreat him for her people" (Esth. 4:8). She responded by reminding him of the law:

> "If any man or woman goes to the king inside the inner court without being called, there is but one law—all alike are to be put to death. Only if the king holds out the golden scepter to someone, may that person live. I myself have not been called to come in to the king for thirty days." (Esth. 4:11)

For Esther, Mordecai's request seemed impossible until she received this reply from him:

> "Do not think that in the king's palace you will escape any more than all the other Jews. For if you keep silence at such a time as this, relief and deliverance will rise for the Jews from another quarter, but you and your father's family will perish. Who knows? Perhaps you have come to royal dignity for just such a time as this." (Esth. 4:13–14)

If you have read the rest of the story, then you know that Esther took that risk to her life and was greeted by Ahasuerus's extended scepter, after which she cleverly arranged a banquet for the king that eventually led to Haman's death, the salvation of her people, and Mordecai's elevation in the kingdom in Haman's place.

In the process, Esther herself was transformed: from her training as a compliant harem girl (although she certainly didn't have much choice in the matter), she became a regent of the land. The final chapters of the book show us a woman who has come into her own as an *ezer* leader.

Sometimes a major challenge can change us completely, a personal transformation that we could never have imagined possible, just as it was for Queen Esther.

 Food for Thought

If your job makes demands on you that seem impossible, what can you do to manage them?

_____

_____

_____

_____

_____

_____

In what ways might God be at work in your job that you may not recognize?

_____

_____

_____

_____

_____

_____

Prayer

Lord,

Like Huldah, help us to speak the truth with wisdom and discernment when and where it is needed. Like Esther, enable us to be brave when called to take a risk for a great purpose. Cause us to see ourselves as an "angled mirror," reflecting your image wherever we are. Give us also the strength to do whatever you call us to do.

Amen.

Chapter 8

Lady Wisdom and the Woman of Strength

Lesson #1: Lady Wisdom (Proverbs 1:20–33)

Some passages of Scripture, in comedian Rodney Dangerfield's immortal words, "just don't get no respect." One such passage is Proverbs 31:10–31. Men tend to ignore it because it's about a woman, and women choose to ignore it because too many sermons have used it to create guilt in them. But there are several reasons why we can't ignore this passage.

First, we can't ignore it because it's in the Bible. The Apostle Paul reminds us that "all scripture is inspired by God and is useful for teaching, for reproof, for correction, and for training in righteousness" (2 Tim. 3:16). Second, we can't ignore it because Proverbs 31:10–31 is embedded in a king's instructions to his courtiers, part of the royal teaching given to some leading men. Third, we can't ignore this passage because it summarizes the wisdom of the people of God throughout the book of Proverbs. Finally, we can't ignore Proverbs 31:10–31 because of its structure. These last twenty-two verses of the book of Proverbs form an acrostic poem: each verse begins with the next letter of the Hebrew alphabet, so that everyone could memorize the passage. It was that important!

The fact that Proverbs 31:10–31 uses a woman as an example of wise living should not surprise us, because from the beginning of the book of Proverbs wisdom is personified in Lady Wisdom. We first meet her in Proverbs 1:20–33. There we find her crying out in the marketplace, telling young men to change their ways. They scoffed at wisdom and knowledge, thinking they didn't need it.

What was their ignorance about? "They hated knowledge and did not choose the fear of the LORD" (Prov. 1:29). Throughout the book of Proverbs, "the fear of the LORD is the beginning of wisdom, and the knowledge of the Holy One is insight" (Prov. 9:10), and Lady Wisdom says that those who listen to her "will be secure and will live at ease, without dread of disaster" (Prov. 1:33).

What is this "fear of the Lord" that permeates the book of Proverbs? It's not terror at the thought of God's power. Rather, it is awe that such a powerful God could love and care for the likes of us. "Fear" in this sense throughout the Bible is about a creature marveling in wonder that he or she could have any reason to be the object of God's love. That love draws out of us a love for such a God, which leads us to want to serve his purposes here on earth.

This was the point of our creation "in the divine image" (Gen. 1:26–28) in the first place. We were created for the high purpose of imaging God's values in our world. We are to do that in all of our relationships and in our stewardship of God's earth through our work. Lady Wisdom calls (Prov. 8–9) to get smart, to understand our purpose in life, and to live in the warmth and security of God's love as his "angled mirrors" in a broken world.

We meet Lady Wisdom again in street clothes in Proverbs 31:10–31. There we get some of the specifics for being those "angled mirrors" of God. While many Christian women see "the Proverbs 31 woman" as an impossible domestic ideal or goal, her story is a fitting conclusion to a study of *ezer* women in the Old Testament, as we will see in the next lesson.

Food for Thought

How would you define "wisdom"?

_____

_____

_____

_____

_____

_____

_____

Why do you think wisdom is personified as a woman?

_____

_____

_____

_____

_____

_____

_____

_____

Lesson #2: The Proverbs 31 Woman (Proverbs 31:10–29)

Proverbs 31:10 asks, "A capable wife who can find? She is far more precious than jewels." If we were reading this verse in other translations, we'd find that this capable woman is called "virtuous" (NKJV), "of noble character" (NIV), or "excellent" (NASB). These translations are all misleading. The fact that these words (*capable, virtuous, noble character, excellent*) are not synonymous should alert us that each falls short of the mark in describing this woman.

The Hebrew word they translate is *chayil*, a common word in the Old Testament (occurring 242 times), which is usually associated with soldiers or armies and translated as *strength, strong*, or *mighty* (as it is earlier in Proverbs 31:3). David's "mighty men" were *chayil* men (2 Sam. 23), and what we learn first about this wise woman in Proverbs 31 is that she has strength. "Valiant" might be an appropriate translation, if we had to limit ourselves to one word. As we follow her in this chapter, we see her strength reflected in her actions: "She girds herself with strength, and makes her arms strong" (Prov. 31:17). She knows it takes strength to act in wise ways, so she "exercises" her moral and compassionate muscles.

This woman of strength is characterized by five attributes in Proverbs 31.

1. *She is trustworthy* (vv. 11–12). Her husband trusts her because he knows that she has his best interests at heart. But that extends to the workplace: do colleagues and bosses know that we have their best interests at heart? If we're not trustworthy, then not much else really matters.

2. *She is shrewd* (vv. 13–18). She chooses her tasks and materials carefully. She thinks ahead (bringing food for her family from far away—not always relying on last-minute

take-out!). She's thoughtful about her work ("considering" that field carefully, and then turning it into a profitable vineyard). She produces "merchandise that is profitable"— items she knows she can sell because they are well made.

3. *She is generous* (vv. 19–20). While English translations make these two verses look unrelated, the Hebrew language ties them together grammatically, telling us that this woman spins and weaves so that she has the means to help the poor and needy.

4. *She is diligent* (vv. 21–25). She provides fully for those in her care (even warm clothes in case of snow in the Middle East!). She operates a successful cottage industry, making linen garments and sashes to sell.

5. *She guards her tongue* (v. 26). "She opens her mouth with wisdom, and the teaching of kindness is on her tongue."

Remember Lady Wisdom in Proverbs 1, crying in the marketplace to young men to change their ways and seek wisdom? Here we see Lady Wisdom in action. The wise person is trustworthy, shrewd, generous, diligent, and guards his or her tongue. While wisdom is personified as a woman throughout the book of Proverbs, her wisdom is for men as well as for women. And though the translators in 31:10 refer to her as a *wife* (probably because verse 11 refers to her husband), the Hebrew word is simply the word for *woman*.

Wisdom is needed in all our daily dealings—at work, at home, or in our wider community. It isn't just an abstract idea. Proverbs 31:10–31 makes wisdom concrete so we can see how it should play out in our lives.

Food for Thought

The woman of Proverbs 31:10–31 is depicted as one of the most competent businesspeople in the Bible. Does it surprise you that this person is a woman? If so, why? Describe your thoughts.

_____

_____

_____

_____

_____

_____

Why do you think Proverbs 1:20–21 says, "Wisdom cries out in the street; in the squares she raises her voice. At the busiest corner she cries out; at the entrance of the city gates she speaks"? What does this mean to you?

_____

_____

_____

_____

_____

Lesson #3: The Woman of Strength (Proverbs 31:30–31)

If we are wise, we will be trustworthy, shrewd in handling life, generous to those in need, diligent in carrying out all of our responsibilities, and we'll guard our tongues. But note this:

Although all of these are *evidence* of this woman's wisdom, they are results, not causes. The cause of her wisdom lies in verse 30: "Charm is deceitful, and beauty is vain, but a woman who fears the LORD is to be praised." This links us back to Lady Wisdom's words in Proverbs 9:10: "The fear of the LORD is the beginning of wisdom, and the knowledge of the Holy One is insight." The baseline for wisdom lies in our "knowledge of the Holy One," our "fear of the LORD."

If we interpret "the fear of the LORD" as being terrified at the thought of God's power, then we've missed the central teaching of Scripture concerning God. As noted in Lesson 1 of this chapter, this "fear" is not "terror" but rather "awe" of God. We stand in awe not only of God's power as sovereign over the cosmos, but also of God's amazing, unending love for us. We cannot fathom that he really cares about us. But he does. In his very essence, God is *love*. That love extends to each of us no matter who we are or what we may have done.

Our relationship with God gives us a different perspective on life. We know what matters. We know what lasts and what passes away, and we choose to live for what is eternal. We bring that perspective to every choice we make—whether or not to be trustworthy, to plan ahead and work with care, to show compassion, to pursue our goals with diligence, or to control our tongues.

But as Lady Wisdom told the young men at the beginning of the book of Proverbs, we *choose* whether or not to be wise. It's up to us to decide how we will handle life. As Ella Wheeler Wilcox writes in her 1916 poem " 'Tis the Set of the Sail—or—One Ship Sails East":

But to every mind there openeth,
A way, and way, and away,
A high soul climbs the highway,
And the low soul gropes the low,
And in between on the misty flats,
The rest drift to and fro.

But to every man there openeth,
A high way and a low,
And every mind decideth,
The way his soul shall go.

One ship sails East,
And another West,
By the self-same winds that blow,
'Tis the set of the sails
And not the gales,
That tells the way we go.

Like the winds of the sea
Are the waves of time,
As we journey along through life,
'Tis the set of the soul,
That determines the goal,
And not the calm or the strife.

It's the set of the sail, not the gale—the "set of the soul, that de-termines the goal." Men and women, singles and married, can all learn from Proverbs 31. In every part of your life, including your workplace, choose to live your life wisely in light of what lasts forever. If you do, you *will* be trustworthy, shrewd, generous, dil-igent, and in control of your tongue. Even more, you'll know the difference between what passes away and what lasts, and you'll give yourself to what lasts for eternity. That's God's formula for living life with skill.

Food for Thought

How have you set the sail of your life?

_____

_____

_____

_____

_____

_____

_____

Do you really know and believe that God loves you relentlessly without end? If so, what difference does that make in how you live each day?

_____

_____

_____

_____

_____

_____

_____

Prayer

Lord,

In these lessons, we've come to see that you've given gifts to your daughters to be ezer women in the workplace. Help and guide them to know how to use those gifts. All of us— both men and women—want to be people of strength in our workplaces. Help us see the possibilities of helping others as your Holy Spirit opens our eyes. We pray this for the sake of the work we're called to do. We also pray that your will might be done on earth—where we work—as it is in heaven.

Amen.

Wisdom for Using This Study in the Workplace

Community within the workplace is a good thing, and a Christian community within the workplace is even better. Sensitivity is needed, however, when we get together in the workplace (even a Christian workplace) to enjoy fellowship time together, learn what the Bible has to say about our work, and encourage one another in Jesus' name. When you meet at your place of employment, here are some guidelines to keep in mind:

- Be sensitive to your surroundings. Know your company policy about having such a group on company property. Make sure not to give the impression that this is a secret or exclusive group.

- Be sensitive to time constraints. Don't go over your allotted time. Don't be late to work! Make sure you are a good witness to the others (especially non-Christians) in your workplace by being fully committed to your work during working hours and doing all your work with excellence.

- Be sensitive to the shy or silent members of your group. Encourage everyone in the group and give them a chance to talk.

- Be sensitive to the others by being prepared. Read the Bible study material and Scripture passages and think about your answers to the questions ahead of time.

These Bible studies are based on the Theology of Work biblical commentary. Besides reading the commentary, please visit the Theology of Work website (www.theologyofwork.org) for videos, interviews, and other material on the Bible and your work.

Leader's Guide

Living Word. It is always exciting to start a new group and study. The possibilities of growth and relationship are limitless when we engage with one another and with God's word. Always remember that God's word is "alive and active, sharper than any double-edged sword" (Heb. 4:12) and when you study his word, it should change you.

A Way Has Been Made. Please know you and each person joining your study have been prayed for by people you will probably never meet who share your faith. And remember that "the LORD himself goes before you and will be with you; he will never leave you nor forsake you. Do not be afraid; do not be discouraged" (Deut. 31:8). As a leader, you need to know that truth. Remind yourself of it throughout this study.

Pray. It is always a good idea to pray for your study and those involved weeks before you even begin. It is recommended to pray for yourself as leader, your group members, and the time you are about to spend together. It's no small thing you are about to start and the more you prepare in the Spirit, the better. Apart from Jesus, we can do nothing (John 14:5). Remain in him and "you will bear much fruit" (John 15:5). It's also a good idea to have trusted friends pray and intercede for you and your group as you work through the study.

Spiritual Battle. Like it or not, the Bible teaches that we are in the middle of a spiritual battle. The enemy would like nothing more than for this study to be ineffective. It would be part of his scheme to have group members not show up or engage in any discussion. His victory would be that your group just passes time together going through the motions of a yet another Bible study. You, as a leader, are a threat to the enemy, as it is your desire to lead people down the path of righteousness (as taught in Proverbs). Read Ephesians 6:10–20 and put your armor on.

Scripture. Prepare before your study by reading the selected Scripture verses ahead of time.

Chapters. Each chapter contains approximately three lessons. As you work through the lessons, keep in mind the particular chapter theme in connection with the lessons. These lessons are designed so that you can go through them in thirty minutes each.

Lessons. Each lesson has teaching points with their own discussion questions. This format should keep the participants engaged with the text and one another.

Food for Thought. The questions at the end of the teaching points are there to create discussion and deepen the connection between each person and the content being addressed. You know the people in your group and should feel free to come up with your own questions or adapt the ones provided to best meet the needs of your group. Again, this would require some preparation beforehand.

Opening and Closing Prayers. Sometimes prayer prompts are given before and usually after each lesson. These are just suggestions. You know your group and the needs present, so please feel free to pray accordingly.

Bible Commentary. The Theology of Work series contains a variety of books to help you apply the Scriptures and Christian faith to your work. This Bible study is based on the *Theology of Work Bible Commentary*, examining what the Bible say about work. This commentary is intended to assist those with theological training or interest to conduct in-depth research into passages or books of Scripture.

Video Clips. The Theology of Work website (www.theologyofwork .org) provides good video footage of people from the marketplace highlighting the teaching from all the books of the Bible. It would be great to incorporate some of these videos into your teaching time.

Enjoy your study! Remember that God's word does not return void—ever. It produces fruit and succeeds in whatever way God has intended it to succeed.

> "So shall my word be that goes out from my mouth;
>   it shall not return to me empty,
>   but it shall accomplish that which I purpose,
>   and succeed in the thing for which I sent it." (Isa. 55:11)

"This commentary was written exactly for those of us who aim to integrate our faith and work on a daily basis and is an excellent reminder that God hasn't called the world to go to the church, but has called the Church to go to the world."

BONNIE WURZBACHER

FORMER SENIOR VICE PRESIDENT, THE COCA-COLA COMPANY

Explore what the Bible has to say about work, book by book.

THE BIBLE AND YOUR WORK
Study Series

HENDRICKSON PUBLISHERS

THEOLOGY OF WORK | PROJECT